I0142835

A SHORT HISTORY OF THE MOSQUE IN MINNESOTA

MELISSA AHO

SECOND
GOLDFISH

First Edition. November 2019

ISBN: 978-1-7342769-0-9 (paperback)
ISBN: 978-1-7342769-1-6 (ebook)

Copyright © 2019 Melissa Aho. All rights reserved.
Copyright photographs © 2019 Melissa Aho. All rights reserved.

Publisher: Second Goldfish LLC
Minneapolis, Minnesota
www.secondgoldfish.com

For any inquiries regarding this book, please email:
melissa@secondgoldfish.com

All rights reserved. No part of this book (text or photographs) may be
reproduced in any form or transmitted by any electronic or mechanical
means, including photocopying, recording, information storage and
retrieval system, without written permission from the author, except
where permitted by law.

SECOND
GOLDFISH

CONTENTS

ACKNOWLEDGMENTS

This book started out years ago as a master's paper in Art History on the beautiful Masjid An-Nur in Minneapolis, Minnesota and a few years late as a chapter on Minnesota mosques in the book *Muslims and American Popular Culture.* What I hope to do in this book is to offer readers a glimpse into the history of the Minnesota mosque and its beautiful and unique architectural styles. This book is not intended to discuss every mosque in Minnesota, but rather to give readers a sampling into the origins and how Minnesota mosques continue to grow and changes as their communities grow and change. I hope that it will also inspire the next generation of researchers who find, as I do, the beauty and wonder in these buildings.

I met many kind and gracious individuals while doing my research on mosques in Minnesota. They gave me tours, let me take photographs, and answered many odd questions in person, via telephone, and email as I was doing my research. Granted I did have a few phone calls and emails that were not returned, but they were few and far between. Interestingly the only time I was questioned about my research was when I was taking photos of a Christian church in Minneapolis on a weekday afternoon. Going back all those many years, I would again like to express my gratitude to Imam Makram El-Amin of the Masjid An-Nur, Arlene El-Amin of the Masjid An-Nur, architect Aly El-Nagdy, Owais Bayunus, President of the Islamic Center of Minnesota (ICM), Dr. Adil Ozdemir of the Muslim-Christian Dialogue Center, University of St. Thomas, Dr. Khalid Sami of the ICM, Kausar Hussein of the ICM, Imtiaz Ali Salemohamed of the Anjuman-E-Asghari, Murtaza Mulla of the Anjuman-E-Asghari, Sheikh Mohammed Raza Rizwani of the Anjuman-E-Asghari, and Father Michael O'Connell and Cindy Keller of the Church of the Ascension. Many thanks go out to Dr. Heather Shirey, Dr. Victoria Young, and Dr. Julie Risser of the University of St. Thomas. Thanks to Dr. Catherine Asher, Dr. Alisa Eimen, Dr. Cynthia Becker, Z. Madkour, H. Kazemi, G. Ettouhami, R. Ettouhami, Richard Amos, Paulette Warren, and Dr. C. Churchill. Thank you to the staff and librarians at the University of St. Thomas O'Shaughnessy-Frey Library; Bio-Medical Library, University of Minnesota; Wilson Library, University of Minnesota; Northwest Architectural Archives, Anderson Library, University of Minnesota; Minnesota Historical Society; and the Minnesota Historical Society Press. Special thanks to my family Carole and Terry Aho, Michelle Aho, Che Aho, Candy Aho, and Ginger Aho. All errors found in this book are my own.

Melissa Aho
Minneapolis, Minnesota
November 2019

To Carole, Terry, Michelle, Che, Candy, and Ginger

ILLUSTRATIONS

Figure 1. Anjuman-E-Asghari copula, Brooklyn Park, Minnesota.

1

INTRODUCTION

What makes a mosque a mosque? Is it just a place where Muslims come together to pray? Does the location or the architectural design matter? Or is it "the hopes, dreams and desires of many people," spoken of by Imam Makram El-Amin at the 2006 groundbreaking ceremony that marked the renovation and expansion of the Masjid An-Nur in Minneapolis, Minnesota? [1] With only one mosque in Minnesota with the traditional dome and minaret, it is obvious that many different elements and choices go into creating a mosque in Minnesota. [2]

The number of mosques in Minnesota grows yearly. From just a handful a few years ago, to six mosques by 1991, to about 30 in 2009, to nearly 50 today, mosques can be found around the state in cities like Duluth, Rochester, and St. Cloud, but most are found in Minneapolis and Saint Paul. [3] There was no definitive list of mosques in Minnesota, as mosques are individual entities. There can be mosques within Islamic centers, mosques without an Islamic center, and Islamic centers with an informal mosque. Prayers can be held in hospitals, businesses, and other areas, but these are not usually considered mosques, whereas student associations at colleges and universities who hold prayers in office space are usually considered mosques, but in reality they usually only have a small space and not a building.[4] There can also be mosques in homes and other areas, which are very small and are not organized or listed with the state of Minnesota as a nonprofit religious organization. The majority of mosques in Minnesota are Sunni mosques, but there are a few Shia mosques.

The majority of Minnesota mosques are constructed to blend into their surrounding neighborhoods, so much so that the casual observer might not even identify them as mosques. However, that changed with the addition of the dome and minaret to the Masjid An-Nur, the first mosque in Minnesota to have a dome and minaret. These architectural editions to the structure gave the building an obvious - even prominent – place in the community.

It is important to understand the evolution of a religious building in a non-traditional area – such as Muslim buildings in predominately Christian locations. There are no local historical traditions guiding the construction of mosques in Minnesota prior to the 1960s, unlike other countries where the tradition of mosque building may go back hundreds of years. There are also no historical traditions of Muslim buildings with domes and minarets in Minnesota.

Mosques in Minnesota can generally be broken down into four different categories:

1. A rented space or home with no physical changes on the space or room

2. A purchased building with no major renovations or changes to the space or room
3. A purchased building, which has been renovated and expanded with major changes
4. The building of a new mosque from the ground up

MINNESOTA ARCHITECTURE

T he state of Minnesota has long been associated with a certain type of people and is often refer- enced in popular culture as housing people of Scandinavian decent – especially individuals with a partic- ular 'ya sure, you betcha' accent.[1] It is also considered to be a land of Lutherans and lutefisk. Early European settlers in Minnesota were mainly Christians and by the mid-1800s their Lutheran, Baptist, Methodist, and Catholic churches dotted the landscape.[2] By the 1880s the first Muslim settlers arrived.[3] There are now more than 5 million people in the state and no longer do people of Scandinavian descent and their churches dominate the landscape. Minnesota's popu- lation is growing and estimates project that the Caucasian population will grow only 9 percent in the next 30 years, whereas the minority population is expected to increase 112 percent.[4] As new immigrants arrive and older immigrant populations gain economic and political clout, new commu- nities are formed and new religious buildings are created from the old. It is estimated that there are currently over 150,000 Muslims in Minnesota with the majority of them living in the Twin Cities area of Minneapolis and Saint Paul.[5]

Architectural styles in Minnesota and the Twin Cities have followed those of other parts of the Midwest and the United States. Because so many mosques are storefront mosques, meaning that they are located in buildings that were designed for other purposes, it's important to be aware of what architectural styles are found in Minnesota. From the first settler's shelter, to the farmhouse and the false-front commercial buildings, buildings in Minnesota have evolved into numerous styles, which include: Greek Revival, Gothic Revival, Italianate, French Second Empire, Eastlake, Victorian Gothic, Queen Anne, Richardsonian Romanesque, Workers Cottage, Commercial Blocks, Midwest Square, Classical Revival, Late Goth Revival, Colonial Revival, Chicago Commercial, Beaux-Arts Classicism (also called the Renaissance Revival or Classical Revival), Arts and Crafts (also called the Craftsman or Bungalow, Mission Style), Period Revival (includes Tutor Revival, Spanish Colonial Revival and French Provincial), Prairie, Art Deco, Modern (also called International Style), Postmodern, and Expressive Modernism styles.[6] Churches and other religious buildings were created in these architectural styles and are often found with unique architectural features such as cupolas, domes, steeples, and towers.[7] Cupolas, steeples, and towers are similar to mosque minarets in that they help mark the location of a religious building, they also help to symbolize the specific religion, and they all have been used as a way to call their congregations to worship. Large mosaic and copper domes on St. Constantine's Ukrainian Catholic Church in Northeast Minneapolis or the copper domes on the Maronite Catholic Church Saint Maron also found in Northeast Minneapolis easily help mark their buildings as

Christian churches. Towers are also easily found in the local landscape, such as those found at Saint Clement in Northeast Minneapolis. No matter what neighborhood you are in, Minneapolis residents are familiar with domes and towers on many religious buildings.

3

A SHORT HISTORY OF THE MOSQUE

W hat "makes a mosque a mosque?" Scholar Robert Hillenbrand has written that "the answer is forbiddingly simple: a wall correctly orientated towards the *qibla*, namely the Black Stone within the Ka'ba in Mecca. No roof, no minimum size, no enclosing walls, no liturgical accessories are required."[1] The original mosque, built in 622 CE, was that of the Prophet Muhammad's house in the ancient city of Medina, in the Hejaz region of what is now Saudi Arabia.[2] As Islam spread across the world, building and design elements from many different cultures were incorporated into the mosque's architecture and certain design elements are now considered standard: the *mihrab* in the *qibla* wall, the *minbar* and facilities for ritual ablutions.[3] Other elements traditionally associated with mosques, but which are not required, may include a demarcated space, the *dikka*, the *kursi*, the *maqsura*, the minaret, and the portal.[4] Scholar Martin Frishman writes, "each region of the Islamic world rapidly evolved a stylistic image of its own, in part at least as a result of local climatic conditions and the availability of building materials combined with related craft skills."[5] Interestingly, during the early Arab conquests, "churches, synagogues, fire temples or *apadanas* were converted into mosques."[6] So the reuse of an existing building, including a religious building, is nothing new to Islamic architectural traditions and continues today with mosques in new areas (such as Minnesota, throughout North America and in Europe) using formerly occupied buildings.[7]

The Dome and Minaret

Both the dome and the minaret's form are architectural innovations that go back hundreds of years before Islam.[8] Early Islamic domes are often associated with audience halls of early Islamic rulers.[9] Islamic art historian Jonathan Bloom writes of an interesting feature of early Islamic architecture: "height was always and exclusively associated with secular architecture, perhaps because palaces were consistently tall buildings in the pre-Islamic near East."[10] Power in architecture was "displayed in terms of horizontal, rather than vertical."[11] Under the Abbasids, the dome became associated with funerary architecture, under the Seljuks a large dome highlight the *qibla* bay the congregational mosque, and the Ottomans used the dome as their prime architectural form in their mosques.[12]

The minaret is often defined as a tower-like structure whose original function was to identify the building as a mosque and "to ensure that the voice of the muezzin making the *adhan* could be heard at a maximum distance."[13] Its argued that the minaret takes its form from Syrian Christian bell towers in Damascus that were transformed into mosques during the Umayyad Dynasty or from Zoroastrian fire-towers or Roman watchtowers or even costal light-houses.[14] There were no minarets on the Prophet Muhammad's house in Medina, there is no mention of the minaret in the Quran, and for many years after the Prophet Muhammad's death minarets were not used.[15] Bloom argues that the origin of the minaret comes not from Umayyad Syria, but a century later in Abbasid Mesopotamia, where the Abbasids consistently built towers attached to their mosques.[16] These Abbasid towers "signaled the growing importance of the congregational mosque as a religious institution and as the center of the *'ulama*, the class of religious scholars that was crystallizing at the time."[17] Bloom suggests that the tower, which would evolve into numerous shapes and heights around the world, were "introduced primarily as a marker or indicator of the presence of Islam, not specifically as a place to give the call to prayer."[18]

Art historian Oleg Grabar writes that early Muslim populations were not restricted to a single area, like in Damascus, but were spread throughout the noisy cities. Utilizing the minaret as a way to call the faithful to prayer would not have worked in these conditions. Rather, Grabar argues that the minaret was "a symbolic expression of the presence of Islam directed primarily at the non-Muslims in the city."[19] Later, in cities like Cairo and Istanbul, perhaps the minaret began to represent "a symbol of social, imperial, or personal prestige or as a purely aesthetic device rather than as the expression of a simple ritual function."[20]

Whatever the origins of the minaret, its idea spread throughout the Islamic world and took many different shapes. Square minarets are found in Palestine, North Africa, Syria, and Spain; cylindrical with exterior stairs are found in Iraq; later, the Ottomans created slim cylindrical and polygonal shafts with conical roofs.[21] Most mosques only have one minaret, but twin minarets were used by the Ottomans and Mughal Empires to signify royal patronage.[22] Four minarets are sometimes found, six are used at the Sultan Ahmet Mosque in Istanbul, and seven minarets are found on a mosque in Mecca.[23] So in essence, the different shapes, styles, and numbers of minarets represent the different traditions and ideas of that society and its history, but they also reflected those individuals that politically and economically supported and funded the building of the mosque and minaret.

4

THE MOSQUE IN THE UNITED STATES

Muslims have been documented in the United States for over 100 years, but it was not until 1965 and the loosening of the American immigration laws that large numbers of Muslims settled in the United States.[1] Early immigrants arrived for economic reasons and did not necessarily intend to settle permanently or to construct mosques.[2] Instead, they used buildings that were created for other purposes, such as abandoned churches, Masonic lodges, fire stations, funeral homes, theaters, warehouses, and shops for their community mosques.[3] Today in the United States, many mosques are built with both regional and international styles and many with are built with domes and minarets. Interestingly, Islamic art historian Jerrilynn D. Dodds finds that in New York domes rather than minarets are the important feature and signify a mosque. The "idea of the dome grew from the community. We believe it makes the mosque more beautiful, more remarkable. You see it and you know it is a mosque... Any new masjid, any community in New York, wants to have a dome...the dome means Muslims in America."[4]

While there are over 1,500 mosques in the United States, a study in 2000 of 1,209 mosques in the United States found that most mosques are relatively young, with 30 percent of them having been established in the 1990s and 32 percent that originated in the 1980s.[5] Interestingly, the study also found that mosques are incredibly diverse - only 7 percent are attended by people of one ethnic group, but almost 90 percent of all mosques have some South Asians, African Americans, and Arabs members of their congregations.[6] Also 64 percent of Muslims in the United States were born in 80 different countries.[7] What this means is that mosques in the United States are ethically mixed, are frequented by people from many different cultures, and that no other country in the world has such a "rich diversity of Muslims" as the United States.[8]

THE FIRST KNOWN MOSQUE IN MINNESOTA

I n the early 1970s an increase of Muslims into the Twin Cities included refugees from Uganda, as well as Muslim students and immigrants from Egypt, India, and Pakistan who attended the University of Minnesota, found jobs in the area, and brought their families here.[1] This group of Muslims, located around the University of Minnesota in Minneapolis, created the first mosque in Minnesota in 1969, called the Dinkytown Mosque.[2] Located in a 'roaming house' or a three-level house in the Dinkytown area on 6th Street, it was a small, cramped space.[3] This brick and wood house was originally built in 1922 and had been turned into an apartment building when the Islamic Center of Minnesota (ICM) purchased it. Members did their own remodeling, knocking down walls and painting them an off white to create a prayer hall that held 35 to 40 people.[4] The carpet was originally green and there was calligraphy and works of art on the walls from India.[5] But the mortgage was too much, even with renting out rooms to students.[6] Luckily for this young group, a letter was sent with an Iranian Dr. Mahmodi who was going back to Saudi Arabia, and somehow this letter made its way to King Faisal; after a phone call from the Saudi Arabian embassy, a check for $35,000 arrived to pay off the mortgage. It was truly "the will of God."[7] But this small mosque soon outgrew its space and the ICM started to look for another building. Eventually the Dinkytown Mosque was sold to another Muslim group, because once a building is made into a mosque, Muslims are obligated to keep it as a mosque.[8]

REUSING A RELIGIOUS SPACE

I n 1976, after seeing how small the Dinkytown Mosque was, a generous backer, Najati Abu Khadra from Saudi Arabia (who had a kidney transplant at the University of Minnesota), provided the funds to purchase an old, unused Mennonite church in the Columbia Heights area – a suburb of Minneapolis, for the members of the Dinkytown Mosque.[1] Initially, opposition to the Muslim presence came from local churches, the surrounding community, and from the Chicago based Mennonite Church, owners of the building. A lawyer was hired, and town meetings were held. Eventually, Abu Khadra was able to purchase the Church for $70,000 on one condition: he also needed to "purchase two houses belonging to the church kitty-corner to the Church building for an additional $50,000."[2] Luckily, the pastor at the nearby church offered to buy the two houses, in order to expand parking for his church's parking lot, and then offered a lease of $1.00 to the Masjid for 99 years. The Columbia Heights Masjid is now called the ICM Abu Khadra Masjid and is operated by the oldest Islamic organization in Minnesota, the Islamic Center of Minnesota (ICM) (Figure 2).[3]

The Islamic Center of Minnesota (ICM) Abu Khadra Masjid kept its original Mennonite architectural shape inside and out, while doing a few renovations to make the space usable as a mosque and for the Muslim community. The interior has the lightwood coloring and exposed beams that give the impression of an upside down ship and which is very reminiscent of many local Christian religious buildings, but the rest of the interior is purely Islamic with calligraphy of Quranic verses on the walls, artwork with Quranic verses, photos of the holy city of Mecca, and a red carpet with a prayer niche design incorporated into the pattern-which is used to line people up during prayer (Figures 3 and 4).[4] There is no *minbar,* instead, a podium is used.

Outside, the yellow and white painted exterior blends into the neighborhood so well that most people passing by would not recognize it as a mosque. The only feature on the exterior of the mosque that signifies that it is an Islamic building is the crescent moon above a window and a sign above the door that reads 'Islamic Center of Minnesota' (Figure 3). For many years the Abu Khadra Masjid was the only mosque in Minnesota to have a *ghusl* room for the ritual cleaning of the dead body.[5]

Figure 2. ICM Abu Khadra Masjid, Columbia
Heights, Minnesota.

Figure 3. Window at the ICM Abu Khadra
Masjid, Columbia Heights, Minnesota.

Figure 4. Prayer area inside the ICM Abu
Khadra Masjid, Columbia Heights,
Minnesota.

Figure 5. Carpet inside the prayer area ICM
Abu Khadra Masjid, Columbia Heights,
Minnesota.

In 1987, the ICM purchased a building and opened a head-
quarters in Fridley, a suburb of Minneapolis, which contains
offices, a school, and a small mosque (Figure 6). While
trying to purchase this building, the ICM once again faced
opposition from members of the local community, including
the local Hindu community.[6] This new building, keeps the
original brick design and shape, and provides a variety of
services for the Muslim community, including marriages,
burials, counseling, and free health care clinic to those in
need.[7]

Starting in 1989, the ICM has the longest established
interfaith dialogue, for meetings of people of all faiths, in
the United States.[8] One case of vandalism to the ICM
Columbia Heights Mosque in 1974 turned into a positive
when local Christian churches called offering their sympa-
thy; a Unitarian Church offered the use of their church for
prayers; and a professor at Bethel College invited Dr. Khalid

Abdus Sami, then head of the ICM, to come and talk to his classes.[9] Dr. Sami would continue to do this for the next 35 years.[10]

Figure 6. ICM, Fridley, Minnesota.

THE FIRST MOSQUE in the northland, and one with a monthly potluck, serving the communities of Northeastern Minnesota, Northwestern Wisconsin and the Upper Peninsula of Michigan is the Islamic Center of Twin Ports (ICTP) in Duluth. For years, the ICTP rented space from the local Christian churches, but with a down payment of $130,000 in 2007 for the Unitarian Universalist Church and after a lot of fundraising, in 2010 they were finally able to pay off the deed to the building with the final $200,000.[11]

7

STOREFRONT MOSQUES

M any Minnesota mosques, such as the Masjid Al Huda (Figure 7) and the Masjid Dawah (Islamic Da'Wah Center) (Figure 8) are in the form of storefront mosques. Storefront mosques come "under the rubric of 'non-pedigreed architecture,' a label designating the 'vernacular, anonymous, spontaneous, indigenous' constructions of the informal, undocumented sector."[1] Once a suitable building is found (usually base on location, the size of the space needed, and what the community can afford), it is purchased and then renovated. Such was the case of the Rochester, Minnesota mosque, the Masjid Abu-Bakr Al-Sidique.[2] The Rochester Muslim community originally prayed in each other's basements and in rooms at the Kahler Hotel, until they finally purchased an American Legion Hall for $200,000 in 1998 and spent $600,000 to renovate it.[3] The Abubakar As-Saddique Islamic Center in Faribault began in 2007 by renting space in strip mall (shopping center) next to a gym and tanning salon, but by 2016 its Somali community purchased a larger one story brick building.[4] The Masjid Al-Huda Mosque in

Minneapolis was another example of a Muslim community finding a building that works for them, in this case a former Jehovah's Witness Hall, which was originally built in 1951 and purchased by the Muslim community in the 1990s for $60,000. Sadly it was destroyed by arson in 1999 and was later located to a new location.[5] The Muslim community of the Abuubakar As-Sadique Islamic Center saved for years to purchase a building in the Phillips neighborhood of Minneapolis for $1.5 million dollars and then renovated it.[6] Founded in 2009, the Abu Huraira Islamic Center in Saint Anthony Village, a suburb of Minneapolis, brought the 4.34 acres lot that was formally the Saint Anthony Business Center for $1,620,000 with a $400,000 down payment in 2012, but due to opposition it was not until 2014 that a final settlement was reached.[7] In recent years, mosques in the cities of Blaine, Plymouth, Willmar, and Bloomington have faced community opposition, but were eventually approved.[8]

Figure 7. Masjid Al Huda, Minneapolis, Minnesota.

Figure 8. Masjid Dawah (Islamic Da'Wah Center), St. Paul, Minnesota.

8

NEW CONSTRUCTION MOSQUES

A few communities have grown enough that have built their own mosques from the ground up. Such is the case of the Anjuman-e-Asghari (Little Community) Masjid in Brooklyn Park (Figure 9), who have the honor of being the first mosque in Minnesota built of totally new construction from the ground up. It is also the first Islamic center built entirely by African immigrants in the United States and is largely composed of East African Indians, Bosnians, Iranians, Pakistanis, Afghans and Iraqis, and the first mosque dedicated to the Shia branch of Islam in Minnesota.[1]

Figure 9. Anjuman-E-Asghari, Brooklyn Park, Minnesota.

THE FIRST DOCUMENTED Shia family came from Uganda in 1972.[2] They were sponsored by a group of Christian churches from the Twin Cities and found only one other East African Shia family in the area. So they, as well as some Sunnis, began to meet in the home of Mullah Hussein Walji for religious occasions.[3] As the community grew larger they rented out the Mounds View Community Center. [4] By 1988 there were about 15 families and a new Shia Islamic Center was needed. With the help of the Shia World Federation and the North American Shia Islamic Communities (NASIMCO), 3.4 acres were purchased in Brooklyn Park, a city which is just north of downtown Minneapolis and which sits on the Mississippi River. After the opening of the Imambara Center with a Masjid in 1989, the community grew quickly. In 1996, they added a *madressah* and in 2003 they were able to add a multipurpose sports complex.[5] The Anjuman e Asghari Masjid would later become the second mosque to offer *ghusi* services to the community.

While this was the first mosque built in Minnesota of new construction, designed by a local architect, it has no dome or minaret and is "virtually indistinguishable from the suburban homes that surround it. To the lay passer-by, the sole indicator of its function as a space for Muslim prayer is the presence of two small metal crescents on the cupolas of the building" (Figures 9 and 1).[6] Inside there are bright white walls and a brown carpet with tape to line the faithful up for prayers. The Anjuman-e-Asghari Masjid does have a *minbar* which sits in the *mihrab* (prayer niche) on the *qiblah* wall (Figure 10). A podium is also included. Art works in the form of photos of the holy city of Mecca and calligraphic short *suras* from the Quran decorate the walls.

Like other mosques, the Anjuman-E-Asghari also experienced vandalism, forcing them to surround their property with a fence. They too are part of an interfaith dialogue. Christian churches in Minnesota sponsored the Anjuman-E-Asghari's earliest families and their Mullah Hussein Walji held talks with Christian congregations and was involved in dialogues with Hindus, Jews, and Christians.

Figure 10. Prayer area with a *minbar* which sits in the *mihrab* (prayer niche) on the *qiblah* wall inside the Anjuman-E-Asghari, Brooklyn Park, Minnesota.

9

BUILDING A DOME AND MINARET

The spiritual history of the Masjid An-Nur (Figure 11 and 12) community goes back to the 1950s with a few African-American families who followed the Elijah Muhammad and The Nation of Islam.[1] Its membership remained relatively small over the next few decades. Then in 1975, Imam Warith Deen Muhammad became leader of The Nation of Islam and changed the organization's direction to "the world wide transitions/practices of Al Islam and the sunnah of Prophet Muhammad Ibn Abdullah (PBUH)" and the Masjid community changed with it; following a more mainstream Sunni approach to Islam.[2]

From the 1950s to the 1970s, the community moved to different locations in North Minneapolis and South Minneapolis.[3] Throughout the years, the name for this Islamic community has also changed from Muhammad Temple, Twin Cities Islamic Study Group, and Masjid Mujaddid.[4] In 1975, members changed from using the term "Temple" to "Masjid," with Imam Warith Deen Muhammad's "transition into the community of Muslims world-wide."[5] The Masjid continues its association with the leadership of Imam Muhammad.

In 1990, the congregation was formally established as the Masjid An-Nur, 'the Masjid of Light.' The congregation was comprised of eight members who rented space in a community center in North Minneapolis.[6] By 1991, their numbers grew to about 75 members and they purchased a building on 8th Avenue North, between Humboldt and Irving Avenues North.[7] In 1993, they obtained their 501(c)(3) tax-exempt status with the Internal Revenue Service.[8] By 1995, the Masjid move again, this time into their current location on Lyndale Avenue.

The neighborhood where the Masjid An-Nur sits was originally settled by Germans and Scandinavians, followed by the Jewish and Black communities. Imam El-Amin says, "Now it's a smorgasbord. We've watched this neighborhood become increasingly diverse."[9] Members of the Masjid's community are mostly African-American, Palestinians, Saudis, and African immigrants.[10] They also run the professional gamut from congressmen to those in education, the medical field, construction workers, taxi drivers, secretaries, salesmen, students, etc.[11] The Masjid An-Nur made history in 2006 when Keith Ellison, one of its members, become the first African American in the history of Minnesota to be elected to the United States Congress and the first Muslim elected to the United States Congress.[12] In 2018 Ellison would go on to become the first African American elected to statewide office in Minnesota as Attorney General and the first Muslim to win a statewide office in the United States.

Figure 11. Masjid An-Nur, Minneapolis,
Minnesota.

LEADERSHIP at the Masjid An-Nur

JUST AS THE Masjid has changed locations in the early days,
it has also changed leaders. Early spiritual leaders included
Charles El-Amin and Rasheed Bilal, but from 1990 to 1996
Matthew Ramadan was the Imam.[13] Ramadan grew up in
the African Methodist Episcopal Church, but found Islam,
he says, because "I was attracted to the overall sense of
equality that I found...Many African-Americans don't find
that in any faith, particularly Christianity. It's the sense of
brotherhood for all people."[14] In 1996 Imam El-Amin was
elected as the youngest Imam at the Masjid An-Nur.[15]

The Masjid An-Nur, like many other mosques in
Minnesota, has a strong sense of community. In 1996 they

received a $100,000 grant from the McKnight Foundation to set up programs that would help their local community.[16] Funding was also received from the Prudential Foundation, American Express, the Walton Foundation, Neighborhood Revitalization Project (NRP), and Hunger Solutions.[17] They created a 'Cooks for Hire' program that ran a six-to-eight week short-order cooking course.[18] They run a monthly food shelf program for needy families, delivering thousands of pounds of non-perishable food items each year and feed a couple of hundred families a year. They also deliver food to the local senior citizen center across the street.[19] Other outreach items for their congregation include classes for youth and adult in Islamic studies, Arabic and prayer classes, and participation in interfaith outreach programs.[20] The Masjid has also received funding from the United States Federal Government to expand community outreach programs for health care screenings and referrals.[21] By receiving funding from local, national, and federal organizations, the Masjid An-Nur is seen to be genuine in their work to help the larger community, thereby giving them the political and economic power to be a positive force in their neighborhood and state.

Imam Makram El-Amin

TO RAISE the money and lead a community through a major building expansion and renovation takes a lot of spirit and leadership; and that fell on the shoulders of Imam Makram El-Amin. Imam El-Amin has been the spiritual leader of the Masjid An-Nur since September 1996.[22]

Born the second of five children to Arlene and Charles

El-Amin in Chicago, he has lived in Minneapolis since 1976.[23] His mother Arlene worked in the National Office of The Nation of Islam in the 1960s; his father was one of the Masjid An-Nur's early Imam's and was one of the Fruit of Islam bodyguards for Elijah Muhammad.[24] His youngest brother is retired professional basketball player Khalid El-Amin.[25] Imam El-Amin graduated from North High School in Minneapolis in 1988 and attended Olive Harvey College in Chicago and the University of Minnesota in Minneapolis.[26] The Imam was part of a 500-member United States delegation that made the Hajj or pilgrimage to the holy city of Mecca, Saudi Arabia in 2003.[27] Besides being a spiritual man and life coach, other jobs included working as a child development technician for the Minneapolis Public Schools, establishing El-Amin Properties in 1997, and co-ownership of The El-Amin's Fish House restaurant in Minneapolis.[28] The Imam and his family have always been part of the North Community.

Imam El-Amin has also become a local and national leader and is often selected to represent American Muslims internationally. In March of 1999, El-Amin was "one of the highly placed Muslims invited to the Vatican...to participate with leaders of other religions, including the Dalai Lama, in a show of ecumenism with the Pope."[29] The Imam called the meeting historical and said that His Holiness Pope John Paul II "wanted wide religious reconciliation."[30] He was a member of the local clergy that met with His Holiness the 14th Dalai Lama on his 2000 visit to Minneapolis.[31] Rabbi Zimmerman of Temple Israel says of the Imam, "He has always been insistent about being a peacemaker."[32] Imam El-Amin is also a member of the Downtown Pastors Association and traveled with other members, including Father Michael O'Connell of Church of the Ascension, in January

2007 to Israel and Palestine.[33] In 2012 the Imam became a American Muslim Civic Leadership Institute Fellow at the University of Southern California, in 2014 he was a Bush Fellowship recipient, and was appointed to be a Chaplain for the Minneapolis Police Department.[34]

The fact that Imam El-Amin is known locally, as having grown up in the North Minneapolis neighborhood, has local business ties, and that his family is known and respected in the community, lends legitimacy and a past to the Masjid. This is something that other mosques in Minnesota, who are usually started by immigrant communities, do not have. The Imam was and is seen as one in the community, helping him gain the political knowhow that paved the way for the Masjid to receive local, national, and federal funds for various community projects. In turn, community involvement helped raise money for the expansion and renovations, and assisted the Masjid's request for building zoning requirements unopposed.[35] No one protested the expansion and renovation of the Masjid An-Nur: no one in the local neighborhood, no one at the City of Minneapolis and no one at the local Catholic Church of the Ascension.[36] This is unique in Minnesota and around the country, as other mosques have had many issues buying property.

Architect Aly El Nagdy

ARCHITECT ALYELDIN (ALY) El-Nagdy was already a member of the Masjid An-Nur, when he heard that the congregation was going to renovate and expand the Masjid.[37] A 1986 graduate of the University of Minnesota's School of Architecture, as well as a 1972 graduate of the University of Cairo in Interior Design, El-Nagdy had ideas of how a mosque should look. He was born, raised, and attended school in Egypt. Later, he would create his college thesis on an Islamic Community Center which included a mosque and school; and he has provided technical assistance to other mosques prior to the renovations at the Masjid An-Nur.[38] El-Nagdy's first full time job was with the Minnesota architectural firm, Birkeland Associates, of Minneapolis, Minnesota, where he worked off and on for a few years, eventually becoming a partner and then president of the firm.[39] Later, upon the death of the founder Harold Birkeland, the firm dissolved and El-Nagdy started his own architectural company under his own name: El-Nagdy Architects.[40] Over the years, Aly El-Nagdy has worked on projects such as schools, community centers, residential housing, office buildings, retail stores, and even a few churches.[41] He is a Minnesota Register Architect, Minnesota Certified Interior Designer, and a Wisconsin Register Architect.[42]

Aly El-Nagdy had assisted the Masjid An-Nur in its various architectural needs since 1993, so he was aware of the Masjid and its user needs.[43] When creating the design for the Masjid An-Nur, El-Nagdy tried to combine both Islamic and modern architectural ideas, as well as design elements that would reflect both the Islamic and American culture.[44]

Architecture of North Minneapolis

North Minneapolis has never been known as a fashionable part of Minneapolis.[45]

The first settlers who arrived in the 1850s built sawmills, lumberyards, factories, and railroads; and the 1870s witnessed the building of houses, churches, commercial buildings, and saloons.[46] From the 1880s to the 1920s developers, "platted numerous subdivisions veering the usual euphonious names, and these were gradually built with single-family homes and a smattering of apartments."[47] Housing styles found in the North neighborhood include vernacular Victorians, modest bungalows, period revival homes, ramblers, ranch houses, and Queen Annes.[48] Behind the Masjid An-Nur, one will find Lynpark, an "in-city suburb with cul-de-sacs and homes that date to the 1970s."[49] Surrounding the Masjid are apartment buildings, a Cub Foods Store, residential homes, and the Franklin Middle School.

The Masjid An-Nur's neighborhood also includes two churches. The Church of the Ascension, which was built in 1902, is located right up the block from the Masjid An-Nur and includes two towers and steeples.[50] These two unsymmetrical towers, one of which is taller and has a finial in the shape of a cross, dominate the neighborhood skyline and are actually taller than the Masjid An-Nur's minaret. Down the block from the Church of the Ascension is the Greater Mount Vernon Missionary Baptist Church, which is also home to a tower and steeple. Religious architecture in the form of tall towers and steeples are nothing new to the Masjid's neighborhood in North Minneapolis, so the minaret, with its tall height, introduces the community to a new architectural form that is part of the Islamic world. It makes the building unique, something recognizable, yet different.

. . .

History of the Building Site

THE HISTORY of the site at Lyndale Avenue goes back to August 1925, when builder J.L. Robinson built a one story 'oil filling station' on the lot for the Standard Oil Company.[51] Then as the years passed, many other commercial buildings resided on this plot of land, including Skip's Bar-B-Que in 1973, a bar and restaurant called Ricks Café Americana in 1982, Porches Restaurant in 1989, and Flamingo Café in 1993.[52]

The original oil filling station was valued at $2,000.[53] Other enterprises would come and go and the building's value would increase and decrease as the years went on. In 1970, the property was in the hands of the Minneapolis Community Development Agency (MCDA) as part of urban renewal program.[54] In 1973, the MCDA basically gave the land to Skip's Bar-B-Que, a restaurant that years later, "died a lingering death of financial starvation."[55] The building and land went by "default to the Small Business Administration, which turned it over to the MCDA in 1980."[56] Then in 1982, the MCDA leased the land and sold the building to Rick's Café Americana for $1.00.[57] By 1983, the building and property was valued at $169,000.[58] In 1986, the owner of Rick's went broke and it was bought and sold to D.E.M. Inc., who kept the name Rick's Café Americana.[59] But Rick's closed again in February 1987, and the building once more went back to the MCDA.[60] By 1989, the property and building was only valued at $120,000 dollars.[61] The MCDA sold the property, in 1989, to the Fifth Quarter Development Corp. for $1.00 and lent them $150,000 to open a restaurant called Porches, where the building was repaired, remodeled, refurbished, and eventually closed.[62] Then in 1995, the congregation acquired the land and building, which was in need of major renovations.[63] The first area to be renovated was the 40-foot-square prayer room, which was completed in 1997 and later a second renovation was completed in 2008.[64]

What we can see from all these properties located at this site is that investors found this lot a prime location for several businesses. More importantly, the City of Minneapolis and MCDA wanted this location to succeed. Why else would they continue to invest in numerous businesses and arranged for mortgage debts to be lowered and even forgiven?[65]

Figure 12. Masjid An-Nur, Minneapolis, Minnesota.

THE 1997 RENOVATIONS

AFTER THE BUILDING was purchased in 1995 it needed some basic renovations to make the 3,900 square feet building useable as a mosque. With a congregation between 75 to 80 worshipers, a 40-foot-square prayer room was created with white walls and a brilliantly colored rose carpet.[66] This renovation did not add to the existing exterior shape of the building, which remained the same for years until the renovation and expansion in 2008 that added to the structure on the north side of the building.

FINANCING the Masjid

BY THE TIME the renovation and expansion began in 2006, the Masjid had raised $1.5 million dollars. This money came from a variety of sources including: the congregation; fundraising dinners (such as the 2005 Minneapolis Urban League dinner) and other events; through the sale of a few real estate properties; and contributions from other local mosques.[67] Minnesota mosques are very supportive of each other and for the Masjid An-Nur this was demonstrated in 'Masjid An-Nur Day,' an event that took place on May 11, 2007. On 'Masjid An-Nur Day,' fifteen Minneapolis and St. Paul mosques raised money by devoting that Friday *Jumah* prayers and donating the day's collections to the renovation and expansion.[68] Between $50,000 to $60,000 dollars were raised.[69] Besides the financial aspect of 'Masjid An-Nur Day,' the non-financial benefits were greater, as they established and continued to establish excellent relationships with other mosques.[70] Retired professional basketball player, and younger brother to the Imam, Khalid El-Amin hosted another fundraising event at the First Annual Khalid El-Amin Celebrity Basketball weekend.[71] Both NBA and NFL celebrities, helping to support the Masjid and its community outreach efforts, attended the event.[72]

Of the $1.5 million dollars raised for the renovation and expansion, $1 million was used on the 2006 Phase I. The rest will be used on the next building phase.[73] The ongoing need for financial support is a part of any religious organization's business plan. The Masjid An-Nur continues to seek support for its upkeep, its community outreach programs, and projects it wants to add and grow for its congregation.

BUILDING

THE MASJID AN-NUR, like any other building that plans on remodeling or expanding is required to seek permission from the City of Minneapolis. An application was made in 2004 with the City of Minneapolis Department of Community Planning and Economic Development Planning Division, for variances that would permit construction of a minaret and additional parking.[74] When the variance request was put before the Department of Community Planning and Economic Development Planning Division, no one objected to the addition of the minaret, dome or the parking or the renovation and expansion.[75] The Northside Residents Redevelopment Council (NRRC) even wrote a letter to the City of Minneapolis Department of Community Planning and Economic Development Planning Division, stating their support for the variance for the minaret and parking.[76] The

Church of the Ascension, which is down the block from the Masjid, also approved the building of the minaret and the new look for the Masjid.[77]

THE 2006 RENOVATION

IT ALL BEGAN in 2004 when the first meeting for planning for the expansion took place in the basement of the mosque.[78] It was easy to see why the expansion was wanted and needed. Over 250 families attended the pink colored Masjid An-Nur, and the prayer area held only 75 people.[79] An overflow area in the basement allowed more people to join in the Friday prayer, but more space was needed.[80] But why stay in this location? Leaders at the Masjid felt "they should renovate their current building rather than move to a new location."[81] According to Arlene El-Amin, the mosque's director of outreach programs, "We felt that where we were was where we needed to be."[82]

It soon became clear that the main point of the 2006 expansion and renovation project was to make sure that the mosque was readily available and identifiable as a mosque.[83] There were three main objectives the Masjid wished to accomplish:

1. To establish a clearly identifiable Islamic architectural edifice of which its members and the northside community can be proud.
2. To expand the current structure to accommodate its ever increasing worship community, and the outreach programs that it operates.
3. To create an aesthetically attractive and

> functional working environment for its
> members, guests, and members of the
> community.[84]

THE MASJID WANTED to send a message of who they were to the community and to the neighborhood.[85] They wanted to "raise the profile in order to bring a better light to the religion of Islam," said Imam El-Amin.[86] Their main selling point for the renovation and expansion took the form of the dome and minaret.[87] They knew right away that they were "embarking on something that hasn't been done in the Twin Cities," said Arlene El-Amin.[88]

The expansion and renovation of the Masjid An-Nur would add more than 6,000 square feet to "the existing building and included a complete makeover of the existing structure."[89] The enlarged *musallah*, the worship/prayer space, would be expanded to hold 300 people and the renovations would allow another 150 to 175 people in other areas of the building.[90] The expansion and renovation was divided up into three different phases due to the availability of funds. Phase I began in 2006, with the other two phases to be carried out when funds permit.

Groundbreaking for Phase I began on Friday September 8, 2006, and the project was completed with a dedication ceremony on Friday August 24, 2007.[91] The builders merged parts of the original structure with a new building. The commercial kitchen, used by the previous building owners, was the main area that remained from the existing building structure. The renovations and expansions involved a doubling of the prayer (*musallah*) area; the creation of brand new *wudu* (ablution) facilities; new offices; a multi-purpose community room in the basement; and creating a new Islamic architectural façade, by adding the dome and minaret to dramatically define the new space as an Islamic building.[92] These two unique architectural features (the dome and minaret) are often used to identify a mosque in other parts of the world, and no other mosques in Minnesota currently possess these design elements.[93] A sound system was also added throughout the building.[94]

Figure 13. *Musallah* or prayer chamber, Masjid An-Nur, Minneapolis, Minnesota.

BUILDING Materials

ARCHITECTURAL HISTORIAN HENRY GLASSIE writes that the "selection of materials are social and economic as well as environmental," and such was the case with the Masjid An-Nur.[95] The original design for the Masjid An-Nur called for a "beautiful limestone brick façade."[96] However, this was scaled back because it was found to be too expensive, so a compromise was reached and stone finish masonry was chosen because it had a rough surface and had a similar color to limestone (Figure 14).[97] The walls ended up being 16 inches thick to help support a proposed 2nd level, which was not added.[98]

Figure 14. *Mihrab*, exterior, Masjid An-Nur, Minneapolis, Minnesota.

THE COLORS of the interior and exterior were a collaborative effort by architect Aly El-Nagdy and a committee at the Masjid.[99] It was the committee that suggested the blue coloring around the minaret and at the base of the dome.[100] El-Nagdy suggested the yellow of the mosque and the committee approved.[101] There is no significance to any of the color choices for the Masjid. Colors were chosen because people liked them. Inside the *musallah*, a white paint was chosen.[102] White was a wise choice, as it makes the room seem bigger and brighter, and when the calligraphic design elements are added, they will stand out; additionally, white is an inexpensive color to purchase.[103] Carpet and wood floors were added throughout the building, including a specially made carpet for the prayer chamber.[104]

Musallah

THE *MUSALLAH* or the prayer area covers the largest area in the Masjid and will hold 300 people (Figure 13).[105] A large room, it has an eight-sided dome with four windows on the dome base. Originally, each side of the dome was to have its own window, but this plan was scaled back to four windows on every other side.[106] While the windows in the dome allow natural light to stream in, there are also numerous recessed lights in the ceiling.

Men and women enter the *musallah* in two separate double door entrances (there is also another side entrance). Once inside the doors, the worshiper's attention is drawn towards the northeast side of the building and toward the *qibla* wall and the *mihrab*. The *qibla* wall points the congregation towards Mecca. It is here, also, where the Imam leads the congregation in prayers. There is no *minbar* at the Masjid An-Nur, but one could certainly be added. Instead, the Imam uses a podium when he talks to the congregation.

One of the "most common motifs of mosque decoration was the writing of a variety of Arabic Texts, mostly Koranic...."[107] Sixteen framed works of art surround the *musallah*, most of which were received as gifts.[108] Some of the art pieces take the form of calligraphy with short *suras* from the Quran and others include the 99 names of the Prophet Muhammad.[109] The importance of having pieces of art with calligraphy and inscriptions from the Quran cannot be emphasized enough. As scholar Wheeler M. Thackston writes, "The Qur'an, or any part thereof, in and on a mosque provides the viewer with a message and focus of mediation. It may incidentally be ornamental or decorative, but a Qur'anic inscription has value in and of itself." [110]

Figure 15. Carpet in the *musallah* or prayer chamber, Masjid An-Nur, Minneapolis, Minnesota.

THE CARPET IS a golden color with numerous prayer niches outline in red, spaced in parallel rows across the *musallah* (Figure 13). The lining of worshipers in parallel rows is found in all mosques, as the "Muslim prayer, *salah*, is a well defined ritual. It has to be performed in parallel rows, in order to follow the movements of the Imam and to face Mecca."[111] When affordable, newer mosques contain specially designed carpets that encourage people to arrange themselves in neat lines. In some mosques, tape in long strips is applied to the floor/carpet to achieve this result; and in older mosques, string hanging above the heads of worshipers or along the ground is used.[112] The prayer niche motif is a common one, found on carpets and rugs for prayers across the Islamic world. When the committee consulted with the carpet manufacturer Ahmed Salama, a Muslim from Georgia, and asked for a bid, the gentleman requested the floor plans and photos of the building.[113] He then surprised the Masjid by telling them the carpet, valued around $15,000 to $20,000, would be donated to the Masjid and the Masjid only had to pay for shipping.[114] The donation of monies towards a carpet or the donation of a whole carpet to a mosque is fairly common, as is occasionally giving a special fee or price for a carpet that is going inside a mosque.[115] The Masjid An-Nur was told that the person donated the carpet "with the hopes of receiving blessings from Almighty God."[116]

THE *MIHRAB* and *Qibla* Wall

THE *MIHRAB*, a concave niche, is usually decorated and is found on the wall of the mosque directed towards Mecca

(Figure 16).[117] Some scholars believe that it originated from the apse found in Christian churches.[118] *Mihrabs* may be rectangular, polygonal or semi-circular in shape and at most mosques there is usually just one.[119] At the Masjid An-Nur the *mihrab* and *qibla* wall are located on the northeast side of the building and are white in color. It is not a traditional concave niche, but instead it is created out of the building's architectural element which carries through from outside (Figure 14). On either side of the *mihrab* are three long windows. These also help to illuminate the area with natural light. They are traditional looking and help to mix a more historic design element with a modern design element; and were also chosen to survive the rain and snow.[120]

Figure 16. *Qibla wall and mihrab,* Masjid An-Nur, Minneapolis, Minnesota.

FROM THE OUTSIDE, the *mihrab* and *minaret* are located right on the corner are the most visible corner on the property. As required, they face Mecca. From the outside, these two architectural features create a unique and beautiful focus point for the building.

ABLUTIONS FOUNTAIN

MUSLIM PRAYERS REQUIRE a ritual washing of the hands and feet, so every mosque should have some type of ablution fountain. Art historian Grabar writes there is "no early information about the place for ablutions in the mosque. It seems fairly certain that ritual cleansing did not take place within the precinct of the mosque until considerably later and it is only then that a monumental form was given to a patently early liturgical requirement."[121] It is believed to have been invented by the Caliph Omar and usually takes the form of a fountain or pool, some quite elaborate and beautifully decorated, and usually located in the *sahn,* courtyard or a side entrance of a mosque.[122] Today, when space allows, it takes the form of a separate room (separate from the bathroom and separate for each of the sexes).

At the Masjid An-Nur the ablution fountain or the *wudu* areas are in the basement. They are two small rooms (one for the men and one for the women) with a few stools to sit on and a few faucets, providing a clean and private area to perform this ritual function (Figure 17).

Figure 17. *Wudu* area, Masjid An-Nur,
Minneapolis, Minnesota.

THE WOMEN'S Area

THERE IS no official women's space at the Masjid An-Nur.
The architect did ask the Masjid if they wanted a separate
area and was told no.[123] The response was that it was not
American and the Masjid rejected the separation.[124]
Women do have separate entryways for entering the prayer
area. Entering separately is a traditional element and is
found at other Minnesota mosques when the space permits
it. The women at the Masjid An-Nur pray in the same space
as the men, but at the back of the *musallah*. By including
both women and men in the prayer area, the Masjid and the
architect combined both American and Islamic building
and cultural traditions to create a building that is functional
for this community.

OTHER AREAS

There are no other traditional Islamic elements, such as a *maqsurah* (an enclosed space near the mihrab for the Imam or the ruler), or the *minbar* (a stairway leading to a small platform) were included.[125] While these elements are more traditional and symbolic, and are often seen in larger, older mosques in other parts of the world, they are not common in Minnesota mosques. This is probably due in part to the small size of Minnesota mosques and the small size of the congregations.

Other areas in the Masjid include offices, bathrooms, and a large hallway in front of the doors to the prayer chamber where worshiper's can place their shoes (which are not allowed in the *musallah*) and hang up their coats.

Exterior

THE EXTERIOR of the building is yellow in color; resembling the limestone color the Masjid originally wanted, but was unable to afford. The *qibla* wall juts out, creating a step-like appearance with a slight opening in the cement blocks (Figure 14). Architect El-Nagdy did this to highlight or tie together the minaret and the *qibla* wall. He wanted to make them a part of the ground, and not part of the building.[126] El-Nagdy says that it was a small idea on a small budget, but he wanted to do something so that they would not seem stuck to the building.[127] On the exterior of the building is a 'Masjid An-Nur' sign, enabling people on Lyndale Avenue to read what building it is.

Phase I also called for the parking lot to be blacktopped.[128] The Masjid received a variance from the City of Minneapolis for parking. This allows the congrega-

tion to park on the streets in the surrounding neighborhood, at the Cub Foods Store, and at the Church of the
Ascension parking lot. Finally, in Phase I of the renovation
and expansion, some basic landscaping was done and little
shrubs were added around the exterior of the Masjid.

The Dome and Minaret

The minaret and dome have long been traditional symbols
of Islamic architecture.[129] When adding them to the Masjid
An-Nur, it was clearly the intention of the Masjid and the
architect to make the building more distinct, to make the
building standout in the surrounding neighborhood, and to
make it a symbol of identification (Figures 18, 19, and 20). [130]

Architect Aly El-Nagdy made numerous drawings of
what he believed the dome and minaret should look like.
Some of the drawings of the minaret took unique and
modern shapes, and some even included balconies. While
the dome is set in place and would be difficult to alter, the
minaret could easily have an outer casing added to change
the shape, as well as a new top ornament, at a later date.

Figure 18. Dome and minaret, Masjid An-Nur, Minneapolis, Minnesota.

Figure 19. Dome, Masjid An-Nur,
Minneapolis, Minnesota.

Figure 20. Minaret of Masjid An-Nur,
Minneapolis, Minnesota.

THE DOME

THE DOME WENT UP on May 8, 2007 during the renovation

and expansion (Figure 19).[131] It is 40 feet in diameter and is octagonal. It rests on a base that was originally proposed to have eight windows, one on each side, but the budget did not permit this and the design was scaled back to include four sides with windows and four sides without the windows.[132] Natural light streams in through these windows. Each of the sides is eight feet long and two feet high, with the actual windows being six feet by two feet.[133] When standing inside the *musallah* and looking out the windows, one only sees sky and a few tree branches.

The dome is made of fiberglass over a metal frame.[134] It was created in pieces and then the pieces were put together by way of an extension joint covered with metal. The color of the dome was created to look like copper.[135] Besides the aesthetic value of the dome, it is also functional in that it adds height in the prayer chamber and it helps with the acoustics, as the voice of the Imam resonates in the room.[136] On top of the dome is a crescent moon finial ornament.

THE MINARET

THE MINARET at the Masjid An-Nur is a long, square shape with a lotus shape ornament on top (Figure 20).[137] It is located in the northeast corner of the building and stands 60 feet tall.[138] The minaret's height was limited because of the surrounding neighborhood zoning laws.[139] The zoning height limit imposed by the city of Minneapolis is 35 feet. It was created from a single steel frame bolted together with plywood and has a stucco finish.[140] It is a non-functioning minaret, in that no one makes the call to prayer from the top and while it is hollow inside, there is no access to the inside or the top.[141]

Minarets are another area where decorations can flourish and the Masjid An-Nur's minaret is no exception, with a blue colored band across the upper portion and a lotus blossom ornament on top. The lotus blossom is formed out of fiberglass.[142] It stands about 6 feet tall and unfortunately was not the shape or proportion desired by the architect.[143] While it can look like a lotus blossom, it is also labeled as an onion on the approved architectural drawings. El-Nagdy hopes to correct this onion shape in one of the next building phases.[144] Exterior lights were placed at the base of the minaret, so that at night the minaret can be illuminated. Because of its inaccessibility, no lights were placed on the top of the minaret.

Due to the height of the minaret, a height variance needed to be requested from the City of Minneapolis, but because there had never been a minaret in Minnesota, the paperwork submitted by the Masjid in support for the height variance reflected standard terminology. In their written statement in request for variance to the City of Minneapolis, the Masjid An-Nur described the "construction of a steeple on the northeast corner of the Masjid consistent with the architecture of the immediate nearby churches. In fact, the Masjid An-Nur steeple would be substantially shorter than the one at the Ascension Church..." and in letters to the Northside Residents Redevelopment Council and Councilperson Natalie Johnson-Lee, the Masjid wrote "height restriction variance for the steeple. City zoning limit is 35 feet. We are requesting 50 feet for the steeple element."[145] By using the term 'steeple' the Masjid was using terminology that the City and others would all recognize, while at the same time providing an idea to the community and city that they would all be familiar with. Interestingly on the City of Minneapolis's approval paperwork the City uses the term minaret.[146]

One of the historical purposes of a minaret was for surrounding neighborhoods to hear the call to prayer, but as the minaret at the Masjid is a non-functioning minaret this does not happen. Because of the acoustics in the building, the Imam can make the call to prayer from his office and be heard throughout the building. The Church of the Ascension, the Masjid's neighbor, still rings their Church bell in the taller north tower before Mass on Saturdays and Sundays and for funerals.[147] The neighborhood is use to hearing a call to the faithful regardless of religion.

The dome and minaret are elements chosen to be simplistic, elegant, and to help claim the building as Islamic, but they also help the building fit into the American culture. Architect Aly El-Nagdy wanted to create something that would be a midway point between the American and Islamic culture and he has succeeded.[148]

10

CONCLUSION

Most mosques in Minnesota fall under the category of vernacular architecture. Vernacular architecture "refers to ordinary buildings and landscapes," it is "architecture that most people build and use, comprising buildings that are commonly encountered."[1] The majority of mosques in Minnesota can be classified as vernacular architecture, because they are housed in ordinary buildings and in ordinary landscapes. But what about the Masjid An-Nur? Prior to the 2006 expansion and renovation, the Masjid An-Nur would certainly fall into the vernacular architecture category, but with the addition of the dome and minaret and the deliberate Islamic design it can no longer be classified as vernacular. It is a beautiful building, set in an ordinary landscape, but it is no longer a building that people would commonly encounter.

Most mosques in Minnesota start out in a rented space and then as their congregation grows and achieves some level of economic, community, and political stability, they purchase a building and land, and later expand on their buildings. As mentioned previously, mosques in Minnesota can generally be broken down into four different categories:

1. A rented space or home with no physical changes on the space or room
2. A purchased building with no major renovations or changes to the space or room
3. A purchased building which has been renovated and expanded with major changes
4. The building of a new mosque from the ground up

What does the future hold for the architectural design of the mosque in Minnesota? Only time will tell. What is certain is that Muslims communities will continue to build mosques according to the needs of their community and with what they have available in terms of economic, community, and political support. This is a pattern long established by other religious communities in Minnesota. So what makes a mosque a mosque? A mosque is more than a building. It is an expression of who the community is and who they want to be.

SUGGESTED READINGS

This book is just the tip of the iceberg on books about mosques, Islamic art and architecture, and Minnesota. For further reading, I would recommend starting with:

Blair, Sheila and Jonathan Bloom. *The Art and Architecture of Islam, 1250-1800*. New Haven, CT: Yale University Press, 1996.

Bloom, Jonathan M. *Minaret: Symbol of Islam*. Oxford, UK: Oxford University Press, 1989.

Bloom, Jonathan and Sheila Blair. *Islamic Arts*. London, UK: Phaidon Press, 1997.

Ettinghausen, Richard, Oleg Grabar and Marilyn Jenkins-Madina. *Islamic Art and Architecture 650-1250*. New Haven, CT: Yale University Press, 2003.

Frishman, Martin and Hasan-Uddin Khan, editors. *The Mosque: History, Architectural Development and Regional Diversity*. London, UK: Thames & Hudson, 2002.

Grabar, Oleg. *The Formation of Islamic Art*. New Haven, CT: Yale University Press, 1987.

Hillenbrand, Robert. *Islamic Art and Architecture*. London, UK: Thames & Hudson, 1998.

Holod, Renata and Hasan-Uddin Khan. *The Mosque and the Modern World: Architects, Patrons and Designs Since the 1950s*. London, UK: Thames and Hudson, 1997.

Millett, Larry. *AIA Guide to the Twin Cities: The Essential Source on the Architecture of Minneapolis and St. Paul*. St. Paul, MN: Minnesota Historical Society Press, 2007.

Lathrop, Alan K. *Churches of Minnesota: An Illustrated Guide*. Minneapolis, MN: University of Minnesota Press, 2003.

Risjord, Norman K. *A Popular History of Minnesota*. St. Paul, MN: Minnesota Historical Society Press, 2005.

NOTES

1. Introduction

1. An Imam is defined as a "leader or any adult male who leads prayers during congregational worship in a mosque" in Martin Frishman and Hasan-Uddin Khan, *The Mosque: History, Architectural Development and Regional Diversity*, (London, UK: Thames and Hudson, 2002), 252; Terry Collins, "Building a New Legacy; As A New Mosque rises in Minneapolis, Twin Cities Muslims Reflect on Their Growing Place here in Post-9/11 America." *Star Tribune*, September 9, 2006.

2. A mosque is the English term for masjid. Throughout this book I will use the term mosque, as that is what most readers will be familiar with and will only use the term masjid when referring to a specific building.

3. Martha Sawyer Allen, "An Islam Primer: Faith Stresses Family, Prayer, Charity" *Star Tribune*, February 10, 1991.

4. Ihsan Bagby, Paul M. Perl and Bryan T. Froehle. *The Mosque in America: A National Portrait:A Report from the Mosque Study Project,* (Washington D.C.: Council on American Islamic Relations, 2001), 2.

2. Minnesota Architecture

1. Marilyn J. Chiat, *America's Religious Architecture: Sacred Places for Every Community.* (New York, NY: John Wiley & Sons, Inc., 1997), 146.

2. Gregg Aamot, *The New Minnesotans: Stories of Immigrants and Refugees* (Minneapolis, MN: Syren Book Company, 2006), 7.

3. Miller, Deborah L. "Middle Easterners: Syrians, Lebanese, Armenians, Egyptians, Iranians, Palestinians, Turks, Afghans." In *They Chose Minnesota: A Survey of the State's Ethnic Groups*, June Drenning Holmquist, editor, 513. St. Paul, MN: Minnesota Historical Society Press, 1981.

4. Martha McMurry, Minnesota Population Projections by Race and Hispanic Origins, 2005-2035. January 2009. http://www.demography.state.mn.us/documents/MinnesotaPopulationProjectionsbyRaceand HispanicOrigin2005to2035.pdf (accessed April 9, 2009).

5. Minnesota Council of Churches. http://mnchurches.org/respectful-

communities/interfaithprogramming/takingheart/MuslimsinMin-
nesota.html (accessed October 13, 2019).

6. Mary Ann Nord, "Minnesota Architecture: Building in Style." *Roots* 11, no. 2 (Winter 1983); Larry Millett, *AIA Guide to the Twin Cities: The Essential Source on the Architecture of Minneapolis and St. Paul* (St. Paul, MN: Minnesota Historical Society Press, 2007), 585-593.

7. Architectural historian Alan K. Lathrop, defines a cupola as "a struc-ture often set on the ridge of a roof, having a domical roof on a square or circular base;" a dome as "a roof formed of rounded vaults or arches on a round base;" a steeple, also called a spire, as the "top of a tower that tapers to a point;" and a tower as a "structure on or beside a church that usually contains the bells and may be capped by a steeple," in *Churches of Minnesota: An Illustrated Guide* (Minneapolis, MN: University of Minnesota Press, 2003), xvii and xix.

3. A Short History of the Mosque

1. Robert Hillenbrand, *Islamic Architecture: Form, Function and Meaning* (New York, MN: Columbia University Press, 1994), 31.

2. Hillenbrand, *Islamic Architecture*, 39.

3. Then *mihrab* is a niche or arch in the wall (the *Qibla* wall) of a mosque that points the direction of the Kaaba in Mecca. The *Qibla* wall also indicates the direction that should be faced when saying prayers. The *minbar* is a pulpit or platform of three or more steps and is used to deliver the Friday prayers. The ritual ablutions are usually performed in a space which has water for washing. Renata Holod and Hasan-Uddin Khan, *The Mosque and the Modern World: Architects, Patrons, and Designs since the 1950s* (London, UK: Thames and Hudson, 1997), 13; Martin Frishman, "Islam and the Form of the Mosque," in *The Mosque: History, Architectural Development and Regional Diversity*, eds. Martin Frishman and Hasan-Uddin Khan (London, UK: Thames and Hudson, 2002), 599.

4. A demarcated space is a "partly roofed and partly open to the sky- to provide accommodation for the congregation at prayer," Frishman, *The Mosque*, 33. The *dikka* is a "raised platform from which the words and actions of the imam are relayed to members of a congregation," Frishman and Khan, *The Mosque*, 282. The *kursi* is a "lectern, espe-cially a stand for a Quran," Ibid. The *maqsura* "an enclosed loge in a mosque formerly used by rulers and dignitaries for privacy and self-protection," Ibid. The portal is the entrance to the mosque, usually part of a massive entrance. Frishman, *The Mosque*, 41.

5. Frishman, *The Mosque*, 41.

6. Dogan Kuban, *Muslim Religious Architecture: Part 1, The Mosque and its Early Development* (Leiden, NL: E. J. Brill, 1974), 14.

7. The first mosque in the United States was the Mother Mosque built in 1934 in Cedar Rapids, Iowa. The Mother Mosque website http://www.mothermosque.org/the-dream/ (accessed October 1, 2019).

8. After the death of the Prophet Muhammad in 632 CE various Islamic dynasties took control of the Islamic world, ruling from different counties and often overlapping each other in time. The main ones include: the Umayyads 661-750 CE, the Abbasids 749-1258 CE, Spanish Umayyads 756-1031 CE, Fatimids 909-1171 CE, Seljuqs 1038-1194 CE, Mamluks 1250-1517 CE, Ottomans 1281-1924 CE, Safavids 1501-1732 CE, and Mughals 1526-1858 CE. Robert Irwin, *Islamic Art in Context: Art, Architecture, and the Literary World* (New York, NY: Harry N. Abrams, Inc., 1997), 258 and 260.

9. Bloom, *Minaret: Symbol of Islam*, 67.

10. Ibid., 66.

11. Ibid., 67.

12. Ibid., 73.

13. Frishman, *The Mosque,* 33.

14. Bloom, *Minaret: Symbol of Islam*, 11; Frishman, *The Mosque,* 41.

15. Jonathan M Bloom, "The Minaret: Symbol of Faith and Power" *Saudi Aramco World* 52, (March/April, 2002), 33.

16. Bloom, *Minaret: Symbol of Islam*, 7; Bloom, *Saudi Aramco World,* 33.

17. Bloom, *Saudi Aramco World*, 33.

18. Ibid., 33.

19. Oleg Grabar, *The Formation of Islamic Art* (New Haven, CT: Yale University Press, 1987), 114.

20. Ibid.

21. Kuban, *Muslim Religious Architecture,* 6 & 7.

22. Frishman, *The Mosque*, 41.

23. Ibid., 41.

4. The Mosque in the United States

1. Omar Khalidi, "Approaches to Mosque Design in North America." In *Muslims on the Americanization Path?,* eds. Yvonne Yazbeck Haddad and John L. Esposito (Atlanta, GA: Scholars Press, 1998), 399.

2. Khalidi, *Muslims on the Americanization Path,* 400.

3. Khalidi, *Muslims on the Americanization Path,* 399; Many religions do this, for example there are at least three synagogues in Minneapolis which were converted into churches after the Jewish populations moved out and into the suburbs.

4. Jerrilynn D. Dodds and Edward Grazda, *New York Masjid: The Mosques of New York City* (New York, NY; PowerHouse Books, 2002), 83 & 84.

5. Ihasn Bagby, Paul M. Perl, and Bryan T. Froehle, *The Mosque in America: A National Portrait: A Report from the Mosque Study Project* (Washington D.C.: Council on American-Islamic Relations, 2001), 3.

6. Ibid.

7. Zahid H. Bukhari, "Demography, Identity, Space: Defining American Muslims" in *Muslims in the United States*, Philippa Strum and Danielle Tarantolo, eds. (Washington DC: Woodrow Wilson International Center for Scholars, 2003), 9.

8. Ibid., 9.

5. The First Known Mosque in Minnesota

1. Khalid Abdus Sami, "The Making of a Minnesota Mosque," *Islamic Center of Minnesota Newsletter* (March 2008), 5.

2. It was not given a different name because it was only meant to be temporary. Dr. Sami, interview with author, April 18, 2009.

3. Sami, *Islamic Center of Minnesota Newsletter*, 5.

4. Sami interview.

5. Ibid.

6. Ibid.

7. Dr. Sami, email to author, April 10, 2009.

8. Ibid.

6. Reusing a Religious Space

1. Sami, *Islamic Center of Minnesota Newsletter*, 5.

2. Ibid., 5.

3. ICM Website, http://www.islamiccentermn.org/icm/user/script_-files/index.asp (accessed January 18, 2009); Miller, *They Chose Minnesota*, 522.

4. Melissa Aho. "Mosques in Minnesota," in *Muslims and American Popular Culture*, eds. Anne R. Richards and Iraj Omidvar (Santa Barbara, CA: Praeger/ABC-CLIO, Inc., 2018), 305-315.

5. Melissa Aho. *Masjid An-Nur: Building Meaning in a Minnesota Mosque.* Master's Paper in Art History (unpublished), University of Saint Thomas, Saint Paul, Minnesota, 2009, 57.

6. Sami interview.

7. Aho, "Mosques in Minnesota."

8. Boudreaux, *Pluralism Project;* Bayunus, interview.

9. Sami interview.
10. Ibid.
11. Islamic Center of Twin Ports (ICTP). http://ictpmn.org; John Lundy "Islamic Center of the Twin Ports Reaches Goal to Pay for Mosque in Woodland." *Duluth News Tribune* August 29, 2010. https://www.duluthnewstribune.com/news/islamic-center-twin-ports-reaches-goal-pay-mosque-woodland; John Hatcher, "Woodland Mosque May Face Forced Closure." *The Statesman*. April 22, 2010. http://www.theumdstatesman.com/blog/2010/04/22/woodland-mosque-may-face-a-forced-closure (accessed October 20, 2019.)

7. Storefront Mosques

1. Susan Slyomovics, "The Muslim World Day Parade and "Storefront" Mosques of New York City" in *Making Muslim Space in North America and Europe.*" ed. Barbara D. Metcalf (Berkeley, CA: University of California Press, 1996), 204.
2. Aamot, *The New Minnesotans*, 107.
3. Ibid., 107.
4. Religions in Minnesota Website. https://religionsmn.carleton.edu/exhibits/show/abubakar as saddique islamic c/locationtime (accessed October 13, 2019).
5. Mary Abbe, "Wellstone inspects Burned Mosque's Ruins" *Star Tribune* March 14, 1999.
6. Terry Collins, "Two Men Sought after fire at Mosque; A Minneapolis City Council Member Called the Blaze Early Thursday a Hate Crime; Police Also Say It Could be Tied to Burglary." *Star Tribune* August 26, 2006.
7. Prather 2014.
8. Yuen, *MPR News*.

8. New Construction Mosques

1. Boudreaux, *Pluralism Project.*
2. Ibid.
3. Ibid.
4. Anjuman-E-Asghari Masjid Website, 2007, http://www.mnjamat.org/JIC-history.htm (accessed February 20, 2009); Boudreaux, *Pluralism Project.*
5. Boudreaux, *Pluralism Project.*
6. Nachiket Chanchani, *Middle East/Middle West.* Master of Art paper

in Art History (unpublished). Minneapolis; University of Minnesota, 2007, 18; Imtiaz Ali Salemohamed, email to author, April 20, 2009.

9. Building a Dome and Minaret

1. Jeffrey Hassan, "Changing the Landscape of Minneapolis: Masjid An-Nur Makes History on Two Fronts" *Muslim Journal*, (September 29, 2006), 3; Masjid An-Nur, *Building Expansion and Renovation Project October 1, 2004*, 2; Imam Makram El-Amin, interview by author, Minneapolis, Minnesota, March 19, 2009.

2. Hassan, *Muslim Journal*, 3.

3. Arlene El-Amin, email message to author, March 31, 2009.

4. Ibid.

5. Masjid An-Nur, *Building Expansion and Renovation Project October 1, 2004*, 2.

6. Allen, *Star Tribune*.

7. Ibid.

8. Masjid An-Nur, *Building Expansion and Renovation Project October 1, 2004*, 2.

9. Peter Leyden, "North Side Area Has a Distinct Past and a Contradictory Present" *Star Tribune,* July 10, 1991; Bill Ward, "Lyndale Avenue: A True Thoroughfare" *Star Tribune,* June 22, 2007.

10. Curt Brown, Dan Browning and Jerry Zgoda, "Day of Prayer in Minnesota: Pleas rise in Cathedral and Mosque" *Star Tribune,* September 15, 2001.

11. Arlene El-Amin, email message, April 13, 2009.

12. Hassan, *Muslim Journal*, 3; Samuel G. Freedman, "Congressman's Imam is Taking a Lead in Interfaith Efforts" *The New York Times* February 10, 2007. When Ellison decided not to run in 2018, Ilhan Omar won Ellison's 5th Congressional District seat with 77.97% of the vote, previously in 2016 she had been the first Somali-American legislator in the United States when she won a seat in the Minnesota House for House District 60B.

13. Matthew Ramadan identified as Imam of Masjid An-Nur in Martha Sawyer Allan, *Star Tribune*; Arlene El-Amin, email message, March 31, 2009.

14. Allen, *Star Tribune*.

15. "For a man to be declared an imam, a panel of eight leaders must agree on his character and knowledge of Islam. Then a congregational vote ratifies the choice" Clark Morphew, "A Vision of Islam/This New Imam, or Leader, is Researching Out to the High-

Crime Neighborhood Surrounding His Mosque in North Minneapolis" *Saint Paul Pioneer Press*, January 5, 1997.

16. Morphew, *Saint Paul Pioneer Press.*

17. City of Minneapolis, Community Planning & Economic Development, Planning Division, "1729 Lyndale Ave N. BZZ-2032" File. Accessed file April 24, 2009.

18. Bill Ward, "Lyndale Avenue: A True Thoroughfare" *Star Tribune.* June 22, 2007; Imam El-Amin, interview.

19. Ibid.

20. Ibid.

21. Jean Hopfensperger, "Faith-Based Grants Flow to Minnesota," *Star Tribune.* June 1, 2004; City of Minneapolis, Community Planning & Economic Development, Planning Division.

22. Masjid An-Nur Website, "Imam Makram El-Amin."

23. Ibid.

24. *Muslim Journal,* "Masjid An-Nur, Minneapolis Dedication;" Freedman, *The New York Times.*

25. Mike McGraw, "Leading Religiously At Early Age, Bulls' El-Amin Learned How to Take Charge" *Daily Herald* December 5, 2000.

26. Masjid An-Nur Website, "Imam Makram El-Amin."

27. Ibid.

28. Masjid An-Nur Website, "Imam Makram El-Amin; Morphew, *Saint Paul Pioneer Press.*

29. Nolan Zavoral, "Pope's Pilgrimage to the Holy Land is Well-Received in Minnesota" *Star Tribune* March 20, 2000.

30. Ibid.

31. Masjid An-Nur Website, "Imam Makram El-Amin."

32. Freedman, *The New York Times.*

33. Father Michael O'Connell, email to author, May 11, 2009.

34. Masjid An-Nur. http://masjidannur.org/about-us/imams-corner/ (accessed October 13, 2019)

35. Jason Wittenberg, Planning Supervisor, City of Minneapolis Department of Community Planning and Economic Development Planning Division. Email to author, April 22, 2009.

36. Father Michael O'Connell email.

37. Hassan, *Muslim Journal,* 3.

38. Aly El-Nagdy, interview by author via telephone, Minneapolis, Minnesota, March 15, 2009; Aly El-Nagdy, interview by author via telephone, Minneapolis, Minnesota, March 24, 2009.

39. El-Nagdy, interview March 24, 2009.

40. Ibid.

41. Masjid An-Nur, *Building Expansion and Renovation Project October 1, 2004*; El-Nagdy, interview March 24, 2009.

42. Masjid An-Nur, *Building Expansion and Renovation Project October 1, 2004.*
43. Masjid An-Nur, *Building Expansion and Renovation Project October 1, 2004.*
44. El-Nagdy, interview March 15, 2009.
45. Millett, *AIA Guide to the Twin Cities,* 288.
46. Ibid., 288.
47. Ibid., 288.
48. Ibid., 288.
49. Ibid., 289.
50. Millett, *AIA Guide to the Twin Cities,* 297; Church of the Ascension Website, http://www.ascensionmpls.org/ (Accessed May 13, 2009).
51. Minneapolis Department of Inspections, Building Permit Index Cards for "1729 Lyndale Ave N, Minneapolis, MN 55411." Northwest Architectural Archives, University of Minnesota, Minneapolis, Minnesota. Accessed March 27, 2009.
52. Jim Fuller, "Plans for New Restaurant Are a Mystery – So's the Motivation" *Star Tribune,* April 29, 1988; Jim Jones, "Bad Checks Tip Balances Against Small Business" *Star Tribune,* March 17, 1989; Minneapolis Property Information, "1729 Lyndale Ave N, Minneapolis, MN 55411. PID: 1602924410154" http://apps.ci.minneapolis.mn.us/PiApp/ (accessed March 22, 2009).
53. Minneapolis Department of Inspections.
54. Fuller, *Star Tribune.*
55. Ibid.
56. Ibid.
57. Ibid.
58. Minneapolis Department of Inspections.
59. Fuller, *Star Tribune*; Jones, *Star Tribune.*
60. Fuller, *Star Tribune.*
61. Minneapolis Department of Inspections.
62. Jones, *Star Tribune.*
63. Clark Morphew, "A Vision of Islam/This New Imam, or Leader, is Researching Out to the High-Crime Neighborhood Surrounding His Mosque in North Minneapolis." *Saint Paul Pioneer Press,* Sunday January 5, 1997.
64. Ibid.
65. The MCDA arranged for "the $500,000 mortgage debt on the property to be settled by the new owners for a total of $7000" in Jones, *Star Tribune.*
66. Morphew, *Saint Paul Pioneer Press.*
67. McKinney, *Star Tribune*; *Muslim Journal,* "Masjid An-Nur, Minneapolis Dedication" August 24, 2007.

68. *Muslim Journal,* "Masjid An-Nur, Minneapolis Dedication."
69. Imam El-Amin, interview.
70. Masjid An-Nur Blog, "Masjid An-Nur Day Follow Up" May 22, 2007, http://www.masjidannur.org (accessed March 18, 2009).
71. *Muslim Journal,* "Masjid An-Nur, Minneapolis Dedication."
72. Ibid.
73. Imam El-Amin, interview.
74. City of Minneapolis, Community Planning & Economic Development, Planning Division.
75. Arlene El-Amin, email message to author, April 13, 2009; Jason Wittenberg, Planning Supervisor, City of Minneapolis Department of Community Planning and Economic Development Planning Division. Email to author, April 22, 2009.
76. City of Minneapolis Community Planning & Economic Development, Planning Division; Arlene El-Amin, email message, April 13, 2009.
77. Arlene El-Amin, email message, April 13, 2009.
78. *Muslim Journal,* "Masjid An-Nur, Minneapolis Dedication."
79. Matt McKinney, "Mosque Prepares Doubling of Space: The Masjid An-Nur Expansion Will Make Room for 300 People in the Prayer Hall." *Star Tribune,* August 1, 2005.
80. McKinney, *Star Tribune.*
81. Ibid.
82. Ibid.
83. Imam El-Amin, interview.
84. Masjid An-Nur, *Building Expansion and Renovation Project October 1, 2004,* 5.
85. Imam El-Amin, interview.
86. McKinney, *Star Tribune.*
87. El-Nagdy, interview March 15, 2009.
88. McKinney, *Star Tribune.*
89. Hassan, *Muslim Journal,* 3.
90. McKinney, *Star Tribune.*
91. Hassan, *Muslim Journal,* 3; *Muslim Journal,* "Masjid An-Nur, Minneapolis Dedication."
92. Masjid An-Nur, *Building Expansion and Renovation Project October 1, 2004,* 1; Hassan, *Muslim Journal,* 3.
93. *Muslim Journal,* "Masjid An-Nur, Minneapolis Dedication."
94. A El-Amin, email message to author, March 31, 2009.
95. Henry Glassie, *Vernacular Architecture* (Bloomington, IN: Indiana University Press, 2000), 29.
96. *Muslim Journal,* "Masjid An-Nur, Minneapolis Dedication."
97. El-Nagdy, interview March 24, 2009.
98. Ibid.

99. Arlene El-Amin, email message to author, March 23, 2009.

100. El-Nagdy, interview March 24, 2009.

101. Ibid.

102. El-Nagdy, interview March 15, 2009.

103. Ibid.

104. Masjid An- Nur Blog, "Masjid An-Nur Day Follow Up."

105. El-Nagdy, interview March 15, 2009.

106. El-Nagdy, interview March 24, 2009.

107. Grabar, *The Formation of Islamic Art*, 128.

108. Arlene El-Amin, email message to author, March 23, 2009.

109. Ibid.

110. Wheeler M. Thackston, "The Role of Calligraphy" in *The Mosque: History, Architectural Development and Regional Diversity*, eds. Martin Frishman and Hasan-Uddin Khan (London, UK: Thames and Hudson, 2002), 43.

111. Kuban, *Muslim Religious Architecture,* 2.

112. Sami interview.

113. Imam El-Amin, interview.

114. Ibid.

115. Ahmed Salama of OW Rugs, phone interview with author, April 29, 2009.

116. Arlene El-Amin, email message to author, April 26, 2009.

117. Grabar, *The Formation of Islamic Art*, 114.

118. Kuban, *Muslim Religious Architecture,* 3.

119. Ibid., 4.

120. Imam El-Amin, interview.

121. Grabar, *The Formation of Islamic Art*, 116.

122. Kuban, *Muslim Religious Architecture,* 9.

123. El-Nagdy, interview March 15, 2009.

124. Ibid.

125. Kuban, *Muslim Religious Architecture,* 3.

126. El-Nagdy, interview March 24, 2009.

127. Ibid.

128. Masjid An-Nur Blog, "Masjid An-Nur Day Follow Up."

129. Hassan, *Muslim Journal*, 3.

130. Imam El-Amin, interview.

131. *Muslim Journal,* "Masjid An-Nur Impacts Minneapolis' Landscape with Muslim Presence" June 1, 2007.

132. El-Nagdy, interview March 24, 2009.

133. Ibid.

134. Ibid.

135. Ibid.

136. Imam El-Amin, interview.

137. El-Nagdy, interview March 24, 2009.
138. El-Nagdy, interview March 15, 2009; El-Nagdy, interview March 24, 2009.
139. El-Nagdy, interview March 15, 2009.
140. El-Nagdy, interview March 24, 2009.
141. Ibid.
142. Ibid.
143. Ibid.
144. El-Nagdy often refers to the shape as an 'onion'. Ibid.
145. City of Minneapolis, Community Planning & Economic Development, Planning Division.
146. Ibid.
147. Father Michael O'Connell email.
148. El Nagdy, interview March 15, 2009.

10. Conclusion

1. Carter and Cromley, *Invitation to Vernacular Architecture,* 8; Vernacular Architecture Forum. "What is Vernacular Architecture." June 24, 2008. http://www.vernaculararchitectureforum.org/learning/whatiu.html (accessed March 29, 2009).

REFERENCES

Aamot, Gregg. *The New Minnesotans: Stories of Immigrants and Refugees.* Minneapolis, MN: Syren Book Company, 2006

Abbe, Mary. "Wellstone Inspects burned Mosque's Ruins." *Star Tribune*, March 14, 1999.

Abu Huraira Islamic Center. Facebook Page, 2019.https://www.facebook.com/pg/abuhurairaic/about/?ref=page_internal (accessed October 13, 2019).

Aho, Melissa. *Masjid An-Nur: Building Meaning in a Minnesota Mosque.* Art History Masters Paper (unpublished), University of Saint Thomas, Saint Paul, Minnesota, 2009.

____. "Mosques in Minnesota," in *Muslims and American Popular Culture*, eds. Anne R. Richards and Iraj Omidvar, 305-315. Santa Barbara, CA: Praeger/ABC-CLIO, Inc., 2018.

Allam, Hannah. "Local Arabs Find Much to Celebrate –

Festivities for Long-Awaited Institute Highlight Arts and Culture Tonight." *Saint Paul Pioneer Press,* April 18, 2003.

Allan, Martha Sawyer. "An Islam Primer: Faith Stresses Family, Prayer, Charity." *Star Tribune,* February 10, 1991.

Anjuman-E-Asghari Masjid Website, 2007 and 2019. http://www.mnjamat.org (accessed February 20, 2009 and October 30, 2019).

El-Amin, Arlene. Email message to Author, March 23, 2009; March 25, 2009; March 31, 2009; April 13, 2009; April 26, 2009.

El-Amin, Imam Makram. Interview by Author. March 19, 2009, Minneapolis, Minnesota.

Amos, Richard. Phone interview by Author. April 2, 2009.

Bagby, Ihsan, Paul M. Perl, and Bryan T. Froehle. *The Mosque in America: A National Portrait: A Report from the Mosque Study Project.* Washington D.C.: Council on American Islamic Relations, 2001.

Bayunus, Owais. Interview by Author. March 15, 2009, Fridley, Minnesota.

Bloom, Jonathan M. *Minaret: Symbol of Islam.* Oxford, UK: Oxford University Press, 1989.

_____. "The Minaret: Symbol of Faith and Power." *Saudi Aramco World* 53, 2002: 26-35.

Boudreaux, Michel. "Anjaman-E-Asghari." *The Pluralism Project at Harvard University*. May 7, 2008. http://pluralism.org/research/profiles/display.php?profile=68796 (accessed March 23, 2009).

Brown, Curt, Dan Browning, and Jerry Zgoda. "Day of Prayer in Minnesota: Pleas rise in Cathedral and Mosque." *Star Tribune,* September 15, 2001.

Bukhari, Zahid H. "Demography, Identity, Space: Defining American Muslims," in *Muslims in the United States*, eds. Philippa Strum and Danielle Tarantolo, 7-20. Washington DC: Woodrow Wilson International Center for Scholars, 2003.

Carter, Thomas and Elizabeth Collins Cromley. *Invitation to Vernacular Architecture: A Guide to the Study of Ordinary Buildings and Landscapes.* Knoxville, TN: The University of Tennessee Press, 2005.

Chanchani, Nachiket. *Middle East/Middle West*. 2007. Art History Masters Paper (unpublished) University of Minnesota, 2007.

Chiat, Marilyn J. *America's Religious Architecture: Sacred Places for Every Community*. NewYork, NY: John Wiley & Sons, Inc., 1997.

Church of the Ascension Website. 2019. http://www.ascensionmpls.org/ (accessed May 13, 2009 and November 11, 2019).

City of Minneapolis Community Planning & Economic

Development, Planning Division. "1729 Lyndale Ave N. BZZ-2032" File. Accessed April 24, 2009.

Collins, Terry. "Two Men Sought After Fire At Mosque; A Minneapolis City Council Member Called the Blaze Early Thursday a Hate Crime; Police Also Say it Could be Tied to Burglary." *Star Tribune*, August 26, 2006.

_____."Building a New Legacy; As A New Mosque rises in Minneapolis, Twin Cities Muslims Reflect on Their Growing Place here in Post-9/11 America." *Star Tribune*, September 9, 2006.

Dodds, Jerrilynn D. and Edward Grazda. *New York Masjid: The Mosques of New York*. New York, NY: Power House Books, 2002.

Freedman, Samuel G. "Congressman's Imam is Taking a Lead in Interfaith Efforts." *The New York Times*, February 10, 2007.

Frishman, Martin. "Islam and the Form of the Mosque." In *The Mosque: History, Architectural Development and Regional Diversity*, eds. Martin Frishman and Hasan-Uddin Khan, 1741. London, UK: Thames & Hudson, 2002.

Frishman, Martin and Hasan-Uddin Khan, editors. *The Mosque: History, Architectural Development and Regional Diversity*. London, UK: Thames & Hudson, 2002.

Fuller, Jim. "Plans for New Restaurant Are a Mystery – So's the Motivation." *Star Tribune,*April 29, 1988.

Glassie, Henry. *Vernacular Architecture.* Bloomington, IN: Indiana University Press, 2000.

Grabar, Oleg. *The Formation of Islamic Art.* New Haven, CT: Yale University Press, 1987.

Hassan, Jeffrey. "Changing the Landscape of Minneapolis: Masjid An-Nur Makes History on Two Fronts." *Muslim Journal*, September 29, 2006.

Hatcher, John. "Woodland Mosque May Face Forced Closure." *The Statesman.* April 22, 2010.http://www.theumd-statesman.com/blog/2010/04/22/woodland-mosque-may-face-aforced-closure (accessed October 20, 2019).

Hillenbrand, Robert. *Islamic Architecture: Form, Function, and Meaning.* New York, NY: Columbia University Press, 1994.

Hirsi, Ibrahim. 2017. "Why Many Young Somali-American Muslims in Minnesota Aren't Going to Mosque." *MinnPost.* June 23, 2017. https://www.minnpost.com/newameri-cans/2017/06/why-many-young-somali-american-muslims-minnesota-arent-goingmosque/ (accessed October 13, 2019).

Holod, Renata and Hasan-Uddin Khan. *The Mosque and the Modern World: Architects, Patrons and Designs Since the 1950s.* London, UK: Thames and Hudson, 1997.

Hopfensperger, Jean. "Faith-Based Grants Flow to Minnesota." *Star Tribune,* June 1, 2004.

_____. "Development displacing a Somali Cultural Asset: A Popular Community Center and Mosque Serving

Minnesota's Largest Somali Neighborhood Will Have to Find a NewHome." *Star Tribune,* April 5, 2007.

Islamic Center of Minnesota (ICM) Website. 2018. http://islamiccentermn.org/ (accessed January 18, 2009 and October 28, 2019).

Islamic Center of Twin Ports (ICTP) Website. http://ictpmn.org (access October 20, 2019).

Islamic Institute of Minnesota Website. http://www.islamicinstituteofmn.com/ (accessed October 16, 2019).

Irwin, Robert. *Islamic Art in Context: Art, Architecture, and the Literary World.* New York, NY: Harry N. Abrams, Inc., 1997.

Jones, Jim. "Bad Checks Tip Balances Against Small Businesses." *Star Tribune,* March 17,1989.

Khalidi, Omar. "Approaches to Mosque Design in North America." In *Muslims on the Americanization Path?,* eds. Yvonne Yazbeck Haddad and John L. Esposito, 399-424. Atlanta, GA: Scholars Press, 1998.

Kuban, Dogan. *Muslim Religious Architecture: Part 1, The Mosque and its Early Development.* Leiden, NL: E. J. Brill, 1974.

Lathrop, Alan K. *Churches of Minnesota: An Illustrated Guide.* Minneapolis, MN: University of Minnesota Press, 2003.

Leyden, Peter. "North Side Area has a Distinct Past and a Contradictory Present." *Star Tribune,* July 10, 1991.

Lundy, John. "Islamic Center of the Twin Ports Reaches Goal to Pay for Mosque in Woodland." *Duluth News Tribune,* August 29, 2010.https://www.duluthnewstribune.com/news/islamic-center-twin-ports-reaches-goal-paymosque-woodland (accessed September 30, 2019).

Masjid An-Nur Blog. "Masjid An-Nur Day Follow Up." May 22, 2007. http://www.masjidannur.org (accessed March 18, 2009).

Masjid An-Nur Website. 2009 and 2019. http://www.masjidannur.org (accessed February 19,2009, March 29, 2009, and November 12, 2019).

Masjid An-Nur. *Building Expansion and Renovation Project October 1, 2004.* (unpublished).

McGraw, Mike. "Leading Religiously at Early Age, Bulls' El-Amin Learned How to TakeCharge." *Daily Herald,* December 5, 2000.

McKinney, Matt. "Mosque Prepares Doubling of Space: The Masjid An-Nur Expansion Will Make Room for 300 People in the Prayer Hall." *Star Tribune,* August 1, 2005.

McMurry, Martha. *Minnesota Population Projections by Race and Hispanic Origins, 2005-2035.* January 2009. http://www.demography.state.mn.us/documents/MinnesotaPopulationProjectionsbyRacendHispanicOrigin2005-to2035.pdf (accessed April 9, 2009).

Miller, Deborah L. "Middle Easterners: Syrians, Lebanese, Armenians, Egyptians, Iranians, Palestinians, Turks,

Afghans." In *They Chose Minnesota: A Survey of the State's EthnicGroups*, June Drenning Holmquist, editor, 511-530. St. Paul, MN: Minnesota HistoricalSociety Press, 1981.

Millett, Larry. *AIA Guide to the Twin Cities: The Essential Source on the Architecture ofMinneapolis and St. Paul.* St. Paul, MN: Minnesota Historical Society Press, 2007.

Minneapolis Department of Inspections. Building Permit Index Cards for "1729 Lyndale Ave N, Minneapolis, MN 55411." Northwest Architectural Archives, University of Minnesota, Minneapolis, Minnesota. Accessed March 27, 2009.

Moffson, Steven H. "Identity and Assimilation in Synagogue Architecture in Georgia, 18701920." In *Constructing Image, Identity, and Place: Perspectives in VernacularArchitecture*, Alison K. Hoagland and Kenneth A. Breisch, editors, 151-165. Knoxville, TN: The University of Tennessee Press, 2003.

Morphew, Clark. "A Vision of Islam/This New Imam, or Leader, is Researching Out to the High-Crime Neighborhood Surrounding His Mosque in North Minneapolis." *Saint Paul Pioneer Press*, Sunday January 5, 1997.

Mother Mosque of American Website. 2019. *http://www.-mothermosque.org/* (accessed October 13, 2019).

Muslim Journal. "Masjid An-Nur Impacts Minneapolis' Landscape with Muslim Presence." June 1, 2007.

_____."Masjid An-Nur, Minneapolis Dedication." August 24, 2007.

El-Nagdy, Aly. Interview by Author. Conducted via telephone March 15, 2009 and March 24, 2009

_____. Unpublished Research. Various drawings, files, and notes of Masjid An-Nur project. Accessed April 5, 2009.

Nord, Mary Ann. "Minnesota Architecture: Building in Style." *Roots*, 11, no. 2 (Winter 1983).

O'Connell, Father Michael. Email to Author, May 11, 2009.

Ohman, Doug. *Churches of Minnesota*. St. Paul, MN: Minnesota Historical Society Press, 2006.

Powell, Joy. "Islamic Funeral Home Gets Burnsville Council OK." *Star Tribune*, May 6, 2008. http://www.startribune.com/islamic-funeral-home-gets-burnsville-council-ok/18713219/(accessed October 13, 2019).

Prather, Sharron. "St. Anthony Mosque Plans are Back on Track." *Star Tribune*, December 22, 2014. http://www.startribune.com/st-anthony-mosque-plans-are-back-ontrack/286632511/ (accessed October 13, 2019).

Risjord, Norman K. *A Popular History of Minnesota*. St. Paul, MN: Minnesota Historical Society Press, 2005.

Salemohaned, Imtiaz Ali. Interview by Author. Conducted March 21, 2009, Brooklyn Center, Minnesota.

_____. Email to Author, April 20, 2009.

Salama, Ahmed of OW Rugs. Interview by Author. Conducted via telephone April 29, 2009.

Sami, Dr. Khalid Abdus. "The Making of a Minnesota Mosque." *Islamic Center of Minnesota Newsletter* (March 2008): 5.

_____. Email to Author, April 10, 2009.

_____. Interview by Author. Conducted via telephone, April 18, 2009.

Serageldin, Ismail, and James Steele. *Architecture of the Contemporary Mosque*. London, UK: Academy Editions, 1996.

Serageldin, Ismail. "Introduction: Regionalism." In *The Mosque: History, Architectural Development and Regional Diversity*, eds. Martin Frishman and Hasan-Uddin Khan, 7275. London, UK: Thames & Hudson, 2002.

Slyomovics, Susan. "The Muslim World Day Parade and "Storefront" Mosques of New York City." In *Making Muslim Space in North America and Europe*, ed. Barbara D. Metcalf, 1-27. Berkeley, CA: University of California Press, 1996, 204-216.

Thackston, Wheeler M. "The Role of Calligraphy." In *The Mosque: History, Architectural Development and Regional Diversity*, eds. Martin Frishman and Hasan-Uddin Khan, 4353. London, UK: Thames & Hudson, 2002.

Vernacular Architecture Forum. "What is Vernacular Architecture." June 24, 2008. http://www.vernaculararchitecture-forum.org/learning/whatis.html (accessed March 29,2009).

Ward, Bill. "Lyndale Avenue: A True Thoroughfare." *Star Tribune*. June 22, 2007.

Williams, Brandt. "Ground broken on million-dollar mosque expansion." *Minnesota Public Radio*. September 8, 2006. http://minnesota.publicradio.org/display/web/2006/09/08/newmosque/ (accessed September 28, 2008).

Wittenberg, Jason. Planning Supervisor, City of Minneapolis Department of Community Planning and Economic Development Planning Division. Email to Author, April 22, 2009.

Woessner, Paula. "Size of Twin Cities Muslim Population Difficult to Determine." *Community Dividend: A Community Development Periodical of the Ninth Federal Reserve District*. August 2002. http://www.minneapolisfed.org/publications_-papers/pub_display.cfm?id=2476 (accessed January 18, 2009).

Yuen, Laura. "After Two Years of Discord, St. Anthony Agrees to Mosque." *MPR News*, December 16, 2014. https://www.mprnews.org/story/2014/12/16/settlement-st-anthonyislamic-center. (accessed October 13, 2019).

Zavoral, Nolan. "Pope's Pilgrimage to the Holy Land is Well-Received in Minnesota." *Star Tribune,* March 20, 2000.

ABOUT THE AUTHOR

Melissa Aho, MA, MEd, MLIS, MS is a librarian, instructor, writer, and entrepreneur. She is currently working on her PhD in International Development at the University of Southern Mississippi. Melissa has published articles, book chapters, over 100 book reviews, and has co-edited a book. She has visited mosques in three different countries (the United States, Egypt, and Guyana).

www.ingramcontent.com/pod-product-compliance
Lightning Source LLC
LaVergne TN
LVHW051354080426
835509LV00020BB/3424